Adult Coloring Book: 31 Soothing Mandala Designs

All illustrations, written content and cover art by Matt Lawrence.
Get in touch with the author by emailing matt@mattlawrence.net.

I0455827

Special thanks to Matt Forney of Mattforney.com and J. Malcolm DeVoy of DevoyLaw.com.

~∾ DEDICATION ∾~

This book is dedicated to each and every person who picks it up. I invite you to sit down, relax, and create your own personal work of art through the magic of coloring. Whether you're already an artist or have never touched a crayon or colored pencil, I hope you find this coloring book to be a soothing, relaxing, and creative experience.

HOW TO USE THIS BOOK

This book contains 31 original, mandala-inspired illustrations, one for each day of the month. Take a bit of time each day to relax and let your creativity flow through you.

Each illustration is different, ranging from simple to complex. Choose any design that catches your eye at this very moment.

Set aside the day's stressful distractions. Find a comfortable chair in a favorite room. Turn off your computer, phone, tablet or any other devices. Ignore text messages and emails. The world can wait for you.

Choose your favorite artistic medium. You can color with crayons, colored pencils, markers or anything else.

There is no right or wrong way to color, so let the soothing coloring experience take you on a journey. Express yourself any way that you want. Color inside the lines, outside the lines or anything in between: this book is yours to create any way you want.

TABLE OF CONTENTS